W9-BNR-768

Contents

Acknowledgments

The publisher would like to thank the companies and organizations listed below for the use of their recipes and photographs in this publication.

American Italian Pasta Company & Makers of Mueller's®, Golden Grain Mission®, R&F®, Martha Gooch®, Ronco®, Anthony's®, Luxury Pasta® and Pennsylvania Dutch Noodles®

Birds Eye Foods

California Wild Rice Advisory Board

Crisco is a registered trademark of The J.M. Smucker Company

Del Monte Corporation

The Golden Grain Company®

Jennie-O Turkey Store®

MASTERFOODS USA

National Pork Board

National Turkey Federation

Reckitt Benckiser Inc.

Unilever

Kick'n Chili

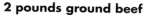

2 pounds ground beef
1 tablespoon *each* salt, cumin, chili powder, paprika, dried oregano and black pepper
2 teaspoons red pepper flakes
2 cloves garlic, minced
¼ teaspoon ground red pepper
1 tablespoon oil
3 cans (about 10 ounces each) diced tomatoes with green chiles
1 jar (16 ounces) salsa
1 onion, chopped

Slow Cooker Directions

1. Combine ground beef, salt, cumin, chili powder, paprika, oregano, black pepper, garlic and ground red pepper in large bowl.

2. Heat oil in large skillet over medium-high heat. Brown beef, stirring to separate meat. Drain and discard fat. Add tomatoes, salsa and onion; mix well. Transfer mixture to slow cooker.

3. Cover; cook on LOW 4 to 6 hours.

Makes 6 servings

Super Chili for a Crowd

2 large onions, chopped
1 tablespoon minced garlic
2 pounds boneless top round or sirloin steak, cut into ½-inch cubes
1 pound ground beef
1 can (28 ounces) crushed tomatoes in purée
1 can (15 to 19 ounces) red kidney beans, undrained
⅓ cup *Frank's® RedHot®* Original Cayenne Pepper Sauce
2 packages (1¼ ounces each) chili seasoning mix

1. Heat *1 tablespoon oil* in 5-quart saucepot or Dutch oven until hot. Sauté onion and garlic until tender; transfer to bowl.

2. Heat *3 tablespoons oil* in same pot; cook meat in batches until well browned. Drain fat.

3. Add *¾ cup water* and remaining ingredients to pot. Stir in onion and garlic. Heat to boiling, stirring. Simmer, partially covered, for 1 hour or until meat is tender, stirring often. Garnish as desired.   *Makes 10 servings*

Chunky Ancho Chili with Beans

5 dried ancho chiles
2 cups water
2 tablespoons vegetable oil
1 large onion, chopped
2 cloves garlic, minced
1 pound boneless beef top sirloin steak, cut into
   1-inch cubes
1 pound boneless pork, cut into 1-inch cubes
1 to 2 fresh or canned jalapeño peppers,* stemmed,
   seeded and minced
1 teaspoon salt
1 teaspoon dried oregano
1 teaspoon ground cumin
½ cup dry red wine
3 cups cooked pinto beans *or* 2 cans (about 15 ounces
   each) pinto or kidney beans, drained

*Jalapeño peppers can sting and irritate the skin, so wear
rubber gloves when handling peppers and do not touch eyes.*

1. Rinse ancho chiles; remove stems, seeds and veins. Place in
2-quart pan with water. Bring to a boil; turn off heat and let
stand, covered, 30 minutes or until chiles are soft. Pour chiles
with liquid into blender or food processor container fitted with
metal blade. Process until smooth; set aside.

2. Heat oil in 5-quart Dutch oven over medium heat. Add onion and garlic; cook until onion is tender. Add beef and pork; cook, stirring frequently, until meat is lightly browned. Add jalapeño peppers, salt, oregano, cumin, wine and ancho chile purée. Bring to a boil. Cover; reduce heat and simmer 1½ to 2 hours or until meat is very tender. Stir in beans. Simmer, uncovered, 30 minutes or until chili has thickened slightly.

Makes 8 servings

Variation: To make chili with chili powder, use ⅓ cup chili powder and 1½ cups water in place of ancho chile purée. Reduce salt and cumin to ½ teaspoon each.

Fireball
Vegetarian Chili

1 onion, chopped
2 cloves garlic, minced
2 cans (15 to 19 ounces each) red kidney beans,
    rinsed and drained
1½ cups *each* **coarsely chopped zucchini and carrots**
  1 can (15 ounces) crushed tomatoes in purée,
    undrained
  1 can (7 ounces) whole kernel corn, drained
  1 can (4½ ounces) chopped green chilies, drained
  ¼ cup *Frank's® RedHot®* **Original Cayenne Pepper**
    Sauce
  1 tablespoon ground cumin

1. Heat *1 tablespoon oil* in large saucepot. Cook and stir onion and garlic 3 minutes or just until tender. Add remaining ingredients; stir until well blended.

2. Heat to boiling. Reduce heat to medium-low. Cook, partially covered, 20 minutes or until vegetables are tender and flavors are blended. Serve with hot cooked rice. Garnish with sour cream or shredded cheese, if desired.   *Makes 6 servings*

Spicy Tomato Chili with Red Beans

1 tablespoon olive oil
1 cup chopped green bell pepper
1 cup chopped onion
1 cup sliced celery
1 clove garlic, minced
1 can (about 16 ounces) red kidney beans, drained and rinsed
1 can (about 15 ounces) diced tomatoes, undrained
1 can (about 10 ounces) diced tomatoes with green chiles
1 can (8 ounces) low-sodium tomato sauce
8 (6-inch) corn tortillas

1. Preheat oven to 400°F.

2. Heat oil in large saucepan over medium heat until hot. Add bell pepper, onion, celery and garlic. Cook and stir 5 minutes or until onion is translucent.

3. Add remaining ingredients except tortillas. Bring to a boil; reduce heat to low. Simmer 15 minutes. Cut each tortilla into 8 wedges. Place on baking sheet; bake 8 minutes or until crisp. Crush half of tortilla wedges; place in bottom of soup bowls. Spoon chili over tortillas. Serve with remaining tortilla wedges.

Makes 4 servings

Hot & Spicy

Cajun Chili

6 ounces spicy sausage links, sliced
4 boneless, skinless chicken thighs, cut into cubes
1 medium onion, chopped
⅛ teaspoon cayenne pepper
1 can (15 ounces) black-eyed peas or kidney beans, drained
1 can (14½ ounces) DEL MONTE® Diced Tomatoes with Zesty Mild Green Chilies
1 medium green bell pepper, chopped

1. Lightly brown sausage in large skillet over medium-high heat. Add chicken, onion and cayenne pepper; cook until browned. Drain.

2. Stir in remaining ingredients. Cook 5 minutes, stirring occasionally. *Makes 4 servings*

Vegetarian Chili

1 tablespoon vegetable oil
1 cup finely chopped onion
1 cup chopped red bell pepper
2 tablespoons minced jalapeño pepper*
1 clove garlic, minced
1 can (28 ounces) crushed tomatoes
1 can (about 15 ounces) black beans, rinsed and drained
1 can (about 15 ounces) chickpeas, rinsed and drained
½ cup corn
¼ cup tomato paste
1 teaspoon sugar
1 teaspoon ground cumin
1 teaspoon dried basil
1 teaspoon chili powder
¼ teaspoon black pepper
Sour cream and shredded Cheddar cheese (optional)

Jalapeño peppers can sting and irritate the skin, so wear rubber gloves when handling peppers and do not touch eyes.

Slow Cooker Directions

1. Heat oil in large nonstick skillet over medium-high heat until hot. Add onion, bell pepper, jalapeño pepper and garlic; cook and stir 5 minutes or until vegetables are tender.

2. Transfer vegetables to slow cooker. Add remaining ingredients except sour cream and cheese; mix well. Cover; cook on LOW 4 to 5 hours. Garnish with sour cream and cheese, if desired.   *Makes 4 servings*

Vegetarian Delights

11

Black Bean Vegetarian Chili

1 tablespoon olive oil
2 onions, finely chopped and divided
1 green bell pepper, diced
1 teaspoon ground cumin
1 teaspoon minced garlic
1 to 2 canned chipotle peppers in adobo sauce,*
   minced
4 cans (about 15 ounces each) black beans, rinsed and
   drained
1 can (about 15 ounces) corn kernels, drained
1 can (about 14 ounces) diced tomatoes, undrained
1 can (6 ounces) tomato paste plus 3 cans water
½ teaspoon salt
½ teaspoon black pepper
   Sour cream

*Chipotle peppers come in 7-ounce cans packed in adobo sauce.

1. Heat olive oil in Dutch oven until hot. Reserve ½ cup chopped onions. Add remaining onions and bell pepper to Dutch oven; cook and stir 5 minutes or until soft. Add cumin; cook and stir about 10 seconds. Add garlic; cook and stir 1 minute.

2. Stir in chipotle peppers, black beans, corn, tomatoes with juice, tomato paste, water, salt and black pepper. Bring to a boil. Reduce heat and simmer 30 minutes.

3. Serve with sour cream and reserved onions, if desired.

Makes 8 servings

Vegetarian Delights

12

Vegetarian Chili with Cornbread Topping

1 pound zucchini, halved and cut into ½-inch slices
1 red or green bell pepper, cut into 1-inch pieces
1 rib celery, thinly sliced
1 clove garlic, minced
2 cans (15 to 19 ounces each) kidney beans, rinsed and drained
1 can (28 ounces) crushed tomatoes in purée, undrained
¼ cup *Frank's*® *RedHot*® Original Cayenne Pepper Sauce
1 tablespoon chili powder
1 package (6½ ounces) cornbread mix, plus ingredients to prepare mix

1. Preheat oven to 400°F. Heat *1 tablespoon oil* in 12-inch heatproof skillet* over medium-high heat. Add zucchini, bell pepper, celery and garlic. Cook and stir 5 minutes or until tender. Stir in beans, tomatoes, **Frank's RedHot** Sauce and chili powder. Heat to boiling, stirring.

2. Prepare cornbread mix according to package directions. Spoon batter on top of chili mixture, spreading to ½ inch from edges. Bake 30 minutes or until cornbread is golden brown and mixture is bubbly.   *Makes 6 servings*

***If handle of skillet is not heatproof, wrap in foil.**

Double-Hearty, Double-Quick Veggie Chili

2 cans (about 15 ounces each) dark kidney beans, rinsed and drained
1 package (16 ounces) frozen bell pepper stir-fry mixture, thawed *or* 2 bell peppers,* chopped
1 can (about 14 ounces) diced tomatoes with peppers, celery and onions
1 cup frozen corn kernels, thawed
3 tablespoons chili powder
2 teaspoons sugar
2 teaspoons ground cumin, divided
1 tablespoon olive oil
½ teaspoon salt
   Sour cream
   Chopped cilantro leaves

If using fresh bell peppers, add 1 small onion, chopped.

Slow Cooker Directions

1. Combine beans, bell peppers, tomatoes, corn, chili powder, sugar and 1½ teaspoons cumin in slow cooker; mix well.

2. Cover; cook on LOW 5 hours or on HIGH 3 hours.

3. Stir in olive oil, salt and remaining ½ teaspoon cumin. Serve with sour cream and cilantro. *Makes 4 to 6 servings*

Chunky Vegetable Chili

2 tablespoons vegetable oil
1 medium onion, chopped
2 ribs celery, diced
1 carrot, diced
3 cloves garlic, minced
**2 cans (about 15 ounces each) Great Northern beans,
  rinsed and drained**
1½ cups water
1 cup frozen whole kernel corn
1 can (6 ounces) tomato paste
1 can (4 ounces) diced mild green chiles, undrained
1 tablespoon chili powder
2 teaspoons dried oregano
1 teaspoon salt

1. Heat oil in large skillet over medium-high heat until hot. Add onion, celery, carrot and garlic; cook 5 minutes or until vegetables are tender, stirring occasionally.

2. Stir beans, water, corn, tomato paste, chiles and liquid, chili powder, oregano and salt into skillet. Reduce heat to medium-low. Simmer 20 minutes, stirring occasionally. Garnish with cilantro, if desired.   *Makes 8 servings*

Vegetarian Delights

15

Vegetable Chili

2 cans (15 ounces each) chunky chili tomato sauce
1 bag (16 ounces) BIRDS EYE® frozen Broccoli, Corn
**   and Red Peppers**
1 can (15½ ounces) red kidney beans
1 can (4½ ounces) chopped green chilies
½ cup shredded Cheddar cheese

• Combine tomato sauce, vegetables, beans and chilies in large saucepan; bring to a boil.

• Cook, uncovered, over medium heat 5 minutes.

• Sprinkle individual servings with cheese.

Makes 4 to 6 servings

Rice and Chick-Pea Chili

⅔ cup **UNCLE BEN'S® ORIGINAL CONVERTED® Brand Rice**
1 can (15 ounces) chick-peas, undrained
1 can (15 ounces) diced tomatoes, undrained
1 can (8 ounces) diced green chilies
1 cup frozen corn
¼ cup chopped fresh cilantro
1 tablespoon taco seasoning
½ cup (2 ounces) shredded reduced-fat Cheddar cheese

1. In medium saucepan, bring 1¾ cups water and rice to a boil. Cover; reduce heat and simmer 15 minutes.

2. Add remaining ingredients except cheese. Cook over low heat 10 minutes. Serve in bowls sprinkled with cheese.

Makes 4 servings

Serving Suggestion: To round out the meal, serve this hearty chili with cornbread and fresh fruit.

Hearty Meatless Chili

1 envelope LIPTON® RECIPE SECRETS® Onion or Onion Mushroom Soup Mix
4 cups water
1 can (16 ounces) chick-peas or garbanzo beans, rinsed and drained
1 can (16 ounces) red kidney beans, rinsed and drained
1 can (14½ ounces) whole peeled tomatoes, undrained and chopped
1 cup lentils, rinsed and drained
1 large rib celery, coarsely chopped
1 tablespoon chili powder
2 teaspoons ground cumin (optional)
1 medium clove garlic, finely chopped

In 4-quart saucepan or stockpot, combine all ingredients. Bring to a boil over high heat. Reduce heat to low and simmer covered, stirring occasionally, 20 minutes or until lentils are almost tender. Remove cover and simmer, stirring occasionally, an additional 20 minutes or until liquid is almost absorbed and lentils are tender. Top with shredded Cheddar cheese, if desired.

Makes about 4 (2-cup) servings

Chicken and Black Bean Chili

1 pound boneless skinless chicken thighs, cut into
   1-inch pieces
2 teaspoons chili powder
2 teaspoons ground cumin
¾ teaspoon salt
1 green bell pepper, diced
1 small onion, chopped
3 cloves garlic, minced
1 can (about 14 ounces) diced tomatoes, undrained
1 cup regular or chunky salsa
1 can (16 ounces) black beans, rinsed and drained
   Optional toppings: sour cream, diced ripe avocado,
   shredded Cheddar cheese, sliced green onions or
   chopped cilantro, crushed tortilla or corn chips

Slow Cooker Directions

1. Combine chicken, chili powder, cumin and salt in slow cooker, tossing to coat. Add bell pepper, onion and garlic; mix well. Stir in tomatoes with juice and salsa. Cover; cook on LOW 5 to 6 hours or on HIGH 2½ to 3 hours or until chicken is tender.

2. Turn heat to HIGH; stir in beans. Cover; cook 5 to 10 minutes or until beans are heated through. Ladle into shallow bowls; serve with desired toppings. *Makes 4 servings*

Shotgun Billy's Turkey Chili with Black Beans

1 can (28 ounces) tomatoes, undrained, coarsely chopped
1 cup coarsely chopped onion
1 red bell pepper, chopped
2 cloves garlic, minced
2 fresh jalapeño peppers,* seeded, minced
1 tablespoon chili powder
1½ teaspoons ground cumin
1½ teaspoons ground coriander
½ teaspoon dried oregano leaves
½ teaspoon dried marjoram leaves
¼ teaspoon crushed red pepper flakes
¼ teaspoon ground cinnamon
2 cups cooked turkey, cut into ½-inch cubes
1 can (16 ounces) black beans, drained, rinsed
½ cup coarsely chopped fresh cilantro
4 tablespoons shredded reduced fat Cheddar cheese

Jalapeño peppers can sting and irritate the skin, so wear rubber gloves when handling peppers and do not touch eyes.

1. Combine tomatoes with juice, onion, bell pepper, garlic and jalapeños in 3-quart microwave-safe dish. Stir in chili powder, cumin, coriander, oregano, marjoram, pepper flakes and cinnamon; cover.

2. Microwave at HIGH (100% power) 10 minutes, stirring once after 5 minutes. Stir in turkey and beans; cover. Microwave at HIGH 4 minutes more or until heated through; stir in cilantro. To serve, ladle into bowls; sprinkle each serving with 1 tablespoon cheese. *Makes 4 servings*

Favorite recipe from **National Turkey Federation**

Tex-Mex Chicken & Rice Chili

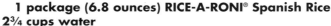

1 package (6.8 ounces) **RICE-A-RONI®** Spanish Rice
2¾ cups water
  2 cups chopped cooked chicken or turkey
  1 can (15 or 16 ounces) kidney beans or pinto beans,
    rinsed and drained
  1 can (14½ ounces) tomatoes or stewed tomatoes,
    undrained
  1 medium green bell pepper, cut into ½-inch pieces
1½ teaspoons chili powder
  1 teaspoon ground cumin
  ½ cup (2 ounces) shredded Cheddar or Monterey Jack
    cheese (optional)
    Sour cream (optional)
    Chopped cilantro (optional)

1. In 3-quart saucepan, combine rice-vermicelli mix, Special Seasonings, water, chicken, beans, tomatoes, green pepper, chili powder and cumin. Bring to a boil over high heat.

2. Reduce heat to low; simmer, uncovered, about 20 minutes or until rice is tender, stirring occasionally.

3. Top with cheese, sour cream and cilantro, if desired.

Makes 4 servings

Chicken Chili

1 tablespoon vegetable oil
1 pound ground chicken or turkey
1 medium onion, chopped
1 medium green bell pepper, chopped
2 jalapeño peppers,* chopped
1 can (28 ounces) diced tomatoes, undrained
1 can (about 15 ounces) kidney beans, drained
1 can (8 ounces) tomato sauce
1 tablespoon chili powder
1 teaspoon salt
1 teaspoon dried oregano
1 teaspoon ground cumin
¼ teaspoon ground red pepper
½ cup (2 ounces) shredded Cheddar cheese

Jalapeño peppers can sting and irritate the skin, so wear rubber gloves when handling peppers and do not touch eyes.

Heat oil in 5-quart Dutch oven or large saucepan over medium-high heat. Cook chicken, onion and bell pepper until chicken is no longer pink and onion is crisp-tender, stirring frequently to break up chicken. Stir in jalapeño peppers, tomatoes with juice, beans, tomato sauce, chili powder, salt, oregano, cumin and red pepper. Bring to a boil over high heat. Reduce heat to medium-low; simmer, uncovered, 45 minutes to blend flavors. To serve, spoon into 6 bowls and top with cheese. *Makes 6 servings*

Santa Fe Skillet Chili

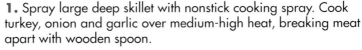

1 to 1¼ pounds ground turkey
1 cup chopped onion
1 teaspoon bottled minced garlic
1 tablespoon chili powder
1 tablespoon ground cumin
¼ to ½ teaspoon ground red pepper
1 can (about 15 ounces) chili beans in spicy sauce, undrained
1 can (about 14 ounces) Mexican- or chili-style stewed or diced tomatoes, undrained
1 can (4 ounces) diced mild green chiles, undrained

1. Spray large deep skillet with nonstick cooking spray. Cook turkey, onion and garlic over medium-high heat, breaking meat apart with wooden spoon.

2. Sprinkle chili powder, cumin and red pepper evenly over turkey mixture; cook and stir 3 minutes or until turkey is no longer pink.

3. Stir in beans with spicy sauce, tomatoes with juice and chiles with liquid. Reduce heat to medium; cover and simmer 10 minutes, stirring occasionally.   *Makes 4 servings*

Serving Suggestion: Offer a variety of toppings with this skillet chili, such as chopped fresh cilantro, sour cream, shredded Cheddar or Monterey Jack cheese and diced ripe avocado. Serve with warm corn tortillas or corn bread.

Three-Bean
Turkey Chili

1 pound ground turkey
1 small onion, chopped
1 can (28 ounces) diced tomatoes, undrained
**1 can (about 15 ounces) chickpeas, rinsed and
    drained**
**1 can (about 15 ounces) kidney beans, rinsed and
    drained**
**1 can (about 15 ounces) black beans, rinsed and
    drained**
1 can (8 ounces) tomato sauce
1 can (4 ounces) diced mild green chiles
1 to 2 tablespoons chili powder

Slow Cooker Directions

1. Cook and stir turkey and onion in medium skillet over
medium-high heat until turkey is no longer pink. Drain fat.
Place turkey mixture into slow cooker.

2. Add remaining ingredients; mix well. Cover; cook on HIGH
6 to 8 hours.   *Makes 6 to 8 servings*

Confetti Chicken Chili

1 pound ground chicken or turkey
1 large onion, chopped
2 cans (about 14 ounces each) reduced-sodium chicken broth
1 can (about 15 ounces) Great Northern beans, rinsed and drained
2 carrots, chopped
1 medium green bell pepper, chopped
2 plum tomatoes, chopped
1 jalapeño pepper,* finely chopped (optional)
2 teaspoons chili powder
½ teaspoon ground red pepper

*Jalapeño peppers can sting and irritate the skin, so wear rubber gloves when handling peppers and do not touch eyes.

1. Heat large nonstick saucepan over medium heat until hot. Add chicken and onion; cook and stir 5 minutes or until chicken is browned. Drain fat.

2. Add remaining ingredients to saucepan; bring to a boil. Reduce heat to low and simmer 15 minutes. *Makes 5 servings*

Santa Fe Turkey Chili

1 tablespoon vegetable oil
1 cup onion chopped
2 cloves garlic chopped
1 tablespoon chili powder
1 (16-ounce) can whole tomatoes, undrained and
    cut-up
1 (15-ounce) can herbed tomato sauce
1 (16-ounce) can red kidney beans, drained
1 cup frozen whole kernel corn
2 cups JENNIE-O TURKEY STORE® Turkey, cooked and
    cubed
¼ teaspoon or to taste cayenne pepper (optional)
    Yogurt, shredded cheese, sliced green onion and
    warm corn tortillas (optional)

In Dutch oven or large saucepan over medium-high heat, heat
oil until hot. Cook onion and garlic until tender. Stir in chili
powder. Add tomatoes with juice, beans and corn. Reduce heat
to low; cover and simmer 10 minutes, stirring occasionally.
Uncover, add turkey and cayenne pepper, if desired; simmer
5 minutes longer. Serve with yogurt, cheese, green onion and
tortillas, if desired. *Makes 6 servings*

Simple Turkey Chili

1 pound ground turkey
1 small onion, chopped
1 can (about 4 ounces) diced mild green chiles
1 can (about 14 ounces) black beans
1 can (about 14 ounces) chickpeas, rinsed and
    drained
1 can (about 14 ounces) kidney beans, rinsed and
    drained
1 can (28 ounces) diced tomatoes, undrained
1 can (8 ounces) tomato sauce
1 to 2 tablespoons chili powder

Cook turkey and onion in Dutch oven over medium-high heat until turkey is no longer pink, stirring with spoon to break up turkey; drain fat. Stir in all remaining ingredients. Bring to a boil. Reduce heat and simmer, stirring occasionally, for about 20 minutes. *Makes 8 servings*

Serving Suggestion: Serve chili over split baked potatoes.

Texas Chili

4 tablespoons CRISCO® Corn Oil*
2 pounds boneless chuck roast, cut into 1-inch cubes
1 large onion, chopped
4 cloves garlic, minced
1 teaspoon cumin
1 tablespoon chili powder
¼ teaspoon crushed red pepper flakes
2 (14½-ounce) cans diced tomatoes
1 (14½-ounce) can beef broth
1 (10-ounce) can enchilada sauce
2 (15-ounce) cans red kidney beans, rinsed and
**   drained**
¼ cup masa harina and ½ cup water, optional
**   Salt and pepper**
3 tablespoons fresh cilantro, minced
½ cup shredded Monterey Jack cheese

Or use your favorite Crisco Oil.

In a large Dutch oven, heat CRISCO Oil over medium-high heat. Add cubed meat in batches, cooking until brown. Add onion and garlic with last batch of meat; drain. Return meat, onion and garlic to the pot. Add cumin, chili powder and crushed red pepper flakes. Stir in tomatoes, beef broth, enchilada sauce and beans; bring to a boil. Reduce heat; simmer, covered, for 1 hour, stirring occasionally. Simmer 30 minutes, uncovered, or until meat is tender. In a small bowl, mix masa harina with water, if desired; stir into chili. Cook 10 to 15 minutes more, stirring frequently. Season to taste with salt and pepper. Garnish with cilantro and shredded cheese.   *Makes 8 servings*

Tasty Beef

Beefy Cajun Chili

1½ pounds ground beef
  **2 cans (about 15 ounces each) Cajun-style mixed
    vegetables, undrained**
  **2 cans (about 10 ounces each) condensed tomato
    soup, undiluted**
  1 can (about 14 ounces) diced tomatoes
  **3 sausages with Cheddar cheese (about 8 ounces), cut
    into bite-size pieces**
  Shredded Cheddar cheese

Slow Cooker Directions

1. Brown beef in large nonstick skillet over medium-high heat, stirring to break up meat. Drain fat.

2. Place ground beef, mixed vegetables with juice, soup, tomatoes and sausages in slow cooker.

3. Cover; cook on HIGH 2 to 3 hours. Sprinkle with cheese.

Makes 10 servings

Grilled Steak Chili

4 tablespoons minced garlic
¼ cup corn oil
3 cups chopped onion
1 can (about 14 ounces) beef broth
3 cans (about 14 ounces each) Mexican-style diced tomatoes with chilies, undrained
2 cans (about 14 ounces each) crushed tomatoes
¼ cup plus 2 tablespoons chili powder
2 teaspoons ground cumin
2 teaspoons dried oregano
1 teaspoon ground black pepper
4 pounds beef steak (preferably ribeye)
¼ cup masa harina (corn flour) or yellow cornmeal (optional)

1. Place garlic and oil in large Dutch oven over low heat. Add onion; cook and stir 5 minutes. Stir in broth, tomatoes with juice, chili powder, cumin, oregano and pepper. Bring to a boil. Stir and reduce heat; cover and simmer 1 to 2 hours or until thick.

2. Preheat grill or broiler. Grill steak about 8 minutes or until just browned on both sides. Let stand 15 minutes. Cut steak into 2×½-inch strips on rimmed cutting board. Stir steak and reserved juices into chili; heat 5 to 10 minutes. For thicker chili, slowly sprinkle in masa harina; cook and stir 12 to 15 minutes or until thickened. *Makes 10 to 12 servings*

Slow Cooker Chili Mac

1 **pound ground beef or turkey**
1 **can (14 ounces) diced tomatoes, drained**
1 **cup chopped onion**
1 **clove garlic, minced**
1 **tablespoon chili powder**
½ **teaspoon salt**
½ **teaspoon ground cumin**
½ **teaspoon dried oregano leaves**
¼ **teaspoon red pepper flakes**
¼ **teaspoon black pepper**
8 **ounces Reduced Carb Elbows (4 cups cooked)**
Grated Cheddar cheese (optional)

1. Brown ground beef in large skillet over medium heat until no longer pink, stirring to break up meat; drain off fat. Place cooked beef in slow cooker with remaining ingredients except elbows and cheese. Mix well. Cook on LOW 4 hours.

2. Cook elbows according to package directions; drain. Stir in cooked elbows and cook on LOW 1 hour more. Top each serving with grated cheese, if desired.   *Makes 10 servings*

Variation: To make this chili on the stovetop, cook elbows; drain. Brown ground beef as in Step 1. Add remaining ingredients except elbows and cheese, and simmer 20 minutes. Stir in elbows. Top each serving with cheese, if desired.

*Favorite recipe from **American Italian Pasta Company***

Chili with Chocolate

- **1 pound ground beef**
- **1 medium onion, chopped**
- **3 cloves garlic, minced and divided**
- **1 can (28 ounces) diced tomatoes, undrained**
- **1 can (about 15 ounces) chili beans in mild or spicy sauce, undrained**
- **2 tablespoons chili powder**
- **1 tablespoon grated semisweet baking chocolate**
- **1½ teaspoons ground cumin**
- **½ teaspoon salt**
- **½ teaspoon black pepper**
- **½ teaspoon hot pepper sauce**

Slow Cooker Directions

1. Cook and stir beef, onion and 1 clove garlic in large nonstick skillet over medium-high heat until beef is browned, stirring to separate meat. Drain fat. Place beef mixture in slow cooker. Add tomatoes with juice, beans with sauce, chili powder, remaining 2 cloves garlic and chocolate; mix well.

2. Cover; cook on LOW 5 to 6 hours. Add cumin, salt, pepper and hot sauce during last 1 hour of cooking.

Makes 4 servings

Easy Chili Con Carne

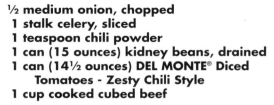

½ **medium onion, chopped**
1 **stalk celery, sliced**
1 **teaspoon chili powder**
1 **can (15 ounces) kidney beans, drained**
1 **can (14½ ounces) DEL MONTE® Diced**
   Tomatoes - Zesty Chili Style
1 **cup cooked cubed beef**

Microwave Directions

1. Combine onion, celery and chili powder in 2-quart microwavable dish. Add 1 tablespoon water.

2. Cover; microwave on HIGH 3 to 4 minutes. Add beans, tomatoes and beef. Cover; microwave on HIGH 6 to 8 minutes or until heated, stirring halfway through cooking time. For a spicier chili, serve with hot pepper sauce.   *Makes 4 servings*

Red & Green No-Bean Chili

4 pounds ground beef chuck (preferably large grind)
2 large onions, chopped
3 banana peppers, seeded and sliced
¼ cup chili powder, or to taste
2 tablespoons minced garlic
1 can (28 ounces) diced tomatoes with green chiles,
    undrained
1 can (about 14 ounces) beef broth
2 cans (4 ounces each) diced mild green chiles,
    drained
2 tablespoons ground cumin
2 tablespoons ground hot paprika
2 tablespoons malt or cider vinegar
1 tablespoon dried oregano
    Hot pepper sauce to taste
    Diced avocado and red onions

1. Brown beef in large Dutch oven over medium heat. Drain fat. Add chopped onions, banana peppers, chili powder and garlic. Reduce heat to medium-low; cook and stir 30 minutes.

2. Add tomatoes, broth, chiles, cumin, paprika, vinegar, oregano and hot pepper sauce. Cook 30 minutes, stirring occasionally. Serve with avocado and red onions. *Makes 8 servings*

Pork and Wild Rice Chili

1 pound boneless pork loin, cut into ½-inch cubes
1 onion, chopped
1 teaspoon vegetable oil
2 cans (14½ ounces each) chicken broth
1 can (18 ounces) white kernel corn, drained
2 cans (4 ounces each) chopped green chilies, drained
¾ cup uncooked California wild rice, rinsed
1 teaspoon ground cumin
½ teaspoon salt
½ teaspoon dried oregano leaves
1½ cups shredded Monterey Jack cheese (optional)
6 sprigs fresh cilantro (optional)

Cook and stir pork and onion in oil in large saucepan over high heat until onion is soft and pork is lightly browned. Add chicken broth, corn, green chilies, wild rice, cumin, salt and oregano. Cover and simmer 45 minutes or until rice is tender and grains have puffed open. Garnish with cheese and cilantro, if desired.

Makes 6 servings

Favorite recipe from **California Wild Rice Advisory Board**

Arizona Pork Chili

    1 tablespoon vegetable oil
1½ pounds boneless pork, cut into ¼-inch cubes
    Salt and black pepper (optional)
    1 can (15 ounces) black, pinto or kidney beans,
      drained
    1 can (14½ ounces) DEL MONTE® Diced Tomatoes with
      Garlic & Onion, undrained
    1 can (4 ounces) diced green chiles, drained
    1 teaspoon ground cumin
    Tortillas and sour cream (optional)

1. Heat oil in large skillet over medium-high heat. Add pork; cook until browned. Season with salt and pepper to taste, if desired.

2. Add beans, tomatoes, chiles and cumin. Simmer 10 minutes, stirring occasionally. Serve with tortillas and sour cream, if desired. *Makes 6 servings*

Country Sausage Chili

2 pounds bulk spicy beef sausage, casings removed
2 green bell peppers, seeded and chopped
2 cups chopped onion
4 cloves garlic, minced
2 cans (28 ounces each) crushed tomatoes
2 cans (4 ounces each) diced mild green chiles, drained
¼ cup ground chili powder
¼ cup molasses
1 tablespoon brown mustard seeds
2 teaspoons red pepper flakes
1 bay leaf
Hot pepper sauce to taste

1. Brown sausage in large Dutch oven over medium heat. Drain fat, leaving 2 tablespoons fat in pot with sausage. Break sausage into chunks. Stir in bell peppers, onion and garlic. Cook and stir 5 to 8 minutes or until onion is translucent.

2. Add tomatoes, chiles, chili powder, molasses, mustard seeds, red pepper flakes, bay leaf and hot sauce. Simmer about 1 hour or until thickened. Remove and discard bay leaf. Serve with biscuits or cornbread, if desired. *Makes 6 to 8 servings*

Winter White Chili

½ **pound boneless pork loin** *or* **2 boneless pork chops,
   cut into ½-inch cubes**
½ **cup chopped onion**
  1 **teaspoon vegetable oil**
  1 **(16-ounce) can navy beans, drained**
  1 **(16-ounce) can chick-peas, drained**
  1 **(16-ounce) can white kernel corn, drained**
  1 **(14½-ounce) can chicken broth**
  1 **cup cooked wild rice**
  1 **(4-ounce) can diced green chilies, drained**
1½ **teaspoons ground cumin**
  ¼ **teaspoon garlic powder**
  ⅛ **teaspoon hot pepper sauce**
   Chopped fresh parsley and shredded cheese

In 4-quart saucepan, sauté pork and onion in oil over medium-high heat until onion is soft and pork is lightly browned, about 5 minutes. Stir in remaining ingredients except parsley and shredded cheese. Cover and simmer for 20 minutes. Serve each portion garnished with parsley and shredded cheese.

Makes 6 servings

Favorite recipe from **National Pork Board**

Chili Verde

½ to ¾ **pound boneless lean pork, cut into 1-inch cubes**
1 **large onion, halved and thinly sliced**
6 **cloves garlic, chopped or sliced**
½ **cup water**
1 **pound fresh tomatillos**
1 **can (about 14 ounces) chicken broth**
1 **can (4 ounces) diced mild green chiles, drained**
1 **teaspoon ground cumin**
1 **can (about 15 ounces) Great Northern beans, rinsed**
   and drained
½ **cup lightly packed fresh cilantro, chopped**
   Jalapeño peppers,* sliced (optional)

**Jalapeño peppers can sting and irritate the skin, so wear
rubber gloves when handling peppers and do not touch eyes.*

1. Place pork, onion, garlic and water in large saucepan.
Cover; simmer over medium-low heat 30 minutes, stirring
occasionally (add more water if necessary). Uncover; boil over
medium-high heat until liquid evaporates and meat browns.

2. Stir in tomatillos and broth. Cover; simmer over medium heat
20 minutes or until tomatillos are tender. Pull tomatillos apart
with 2 forks. Add chiles and cumin.

3. Cover; simmer over medium-low heat 45 minutes or until
meat is tender and pulls apart easily. (Add more water or broth,
if necessary, to keep liquid at same level.) Add beans; simmer
10 minutes or until heated through. Stir in cilantro. Top with
jalapeño peppers, if desired.   *Makes 4 servings*

Hearty Chili Mac

1 pound ground beef
1 can (about 14 ounces) diced tomatoes, drained
1 cup chopped onion
1 tablespoon chili powder
1 clove garlic, minced
½ teaspoon salt
½ teaspoon ground cumin
½ teaspoon dried oregano
¼ teaspoon red pepper flakes
¼ teaspoon black pepper
2 cups cooked macaroni

Slow Cooker Directions

1. Brown ground beef in large nonstick skillet over medium-high heat, stirring to break up meat. Drain fat. Add tomatoes, onion, chili powder, garlic, salt, cumin, oregano, pepper flakes and black pepper. Place in slow cooker; mix well.

2. Cover; cook on LOW 4 hours.

3. Stir in macaroni. Cover; cook 1 hour.   *Makes 4 servings*

Spicy Quick and Easy Chili

1 pound ground beef
1 large clove garlic, minced
1 can (15¼ ounces) DEL MONTE® Whole Kernel Golden
   Sweet Corn, drained
1 can (16 ounces) kidney beans, drained
1½ cups salsa, mild, medium or hot
1 can (4 ounces) diced green chiles, undrained

1. Brown meat with garlic in large saucepan; drain.

2. Add remaining ingredients. Simmer, uncovered, 10 minutes, stirring occasionally. Sprinkle with chopped green onions, if desired. *Makes 4 servings*

Southwest Chili

1 large onion, chopped
1 tablespoon olive oil
2 large tomatoes, chopped
1 can (4 ounces) diced mild green chiles, undrained
1 tablespoon chili powder
1 teaspoon ground cumin
1 can (about 15 ounces) red kidney beans, undrained
1 can (about 15 ounces) Great Northern beans, undrained
¼ cup cilantro leaves, chopped (optional)

Cook and stir onion in oil in large saucepan over medium heat until onion is soft. Stir in tomatoes, chiles, chili powder and cumin. Bring to a boil. Add beans with liquid. Reduce heat to low. Cover and simmer 15 minutes, stirring occasionally. Sprinkle individual servings with cilantro.   *Makes 4 servings*

Easy Slow-Cooked Chili

2 pounds lean ground beef
2 tablespoons chili powder
1 tablespoon ground cumin
1 can (28 ounces) crushed tomatoes in purée, undrained
1 can (15 ounces) red kidney beans, drained and rinsed
1 cup water
2 cups *French's®* French Fried Onions,* divided
¼ cup *Frank's® RedHot®* Original Cayenne Pepper Sauce
Sour cream and shredded Cheddar cheese

*For added Cheddar flavor, substitute French's® Cheddar French Fried Onions for the original flavor.

Slow Cooker Directions

1. Cook ground beef, chili powder and cumin in large nonstick skillet over medium heat until browned, stirring frequently; drain. Transfer to slow cooker.

2. Stir in tomatoes with juice, beans, water, *½ cup* French Fried Onions and **Frank's RedHot** Sauce.

3. Cover; cook on LOW setting for 6 hours (or on HIGH for 3 hours). Serve chili topped with sour cream, cheese and remaining onions. *Makes 8 servings*

Black and White Chili

Nonstick cooking spray
1 pound chicken tenders, cut into ¾-inch pieces
1 cup coarsely chopped onion
1 can (about 15 ounces) Great Northern beans, rinsed and drained
1 can (about 15 ounces) black beans, rinsed and drained
1 can (about 14 ounces) Mexican-style stewed tomatoes, undrained
2 tablespoons Texas-style chili powder seasoning mix

1. Spray large saucepan with cooking spray; heat over medium heat until hot. Add chicken and onion; cook and stir over medium to medium-high heat 5 to 8 minutes or until chicken is browned.

2. Stir beans, tomatoes with juice and seasoning mix into saucepan; bring to a boil. Reduce heat to low; simmer, uncovered, 10 minutes.   *Makes 6 servings*

Serving Suggestion: For a change of pace, this delicious chili is excellent served over cooked rice or pasta.

Quick & Easy

Ragú® Chili

2 pounds ground beef
1 large onion, chopped
2 cloves garlic, finely chopped
1 jar (1 pound 10 ounces) RAGÚ® Robusto®! Pasta Sauce
1 can (15 ounces) red kidney beans, rinsed and drained
2 tablespoons chili powder

In 12-inch skillet, brown ground beef with onion and garlic over medium-high heat; drain. Stir in remaining ingredients. Simmer uncovered, stirring occasionally, 20 minutes. Serve, if desired, with shredded Cheddar cheese and sliced green onions.

Makes 8 servings

Suggestion: For spicier Ragú® Chili, stir in ½ teaspoon each ground cumin and dried oregano.